Payment Methods

By Linda Crotta Brennan

Illustrated by Rowan Barnes-Murphy

The Child's World®

Published by The Child's World®
1980 Lookout Drive • Mankato, MN 56003-1705
800-599-READ • www.childsworld.com

Acknowledgments
The Child's World®: Mary Berendes, Publishing Director
The Design Lab: Design and production
Red Line Editorial: Editorial direction

Design elements: Eric Krouse/Dreamstime

ISBN 9781614732426
LCCN 2012932820

Printed in the United States of America
Mankato, MN
July 2012
PA02122

About the Author

Linda Crotta Brennan has a master's degree in early childhood education. She has taught elementary school and worked in a library. Now, she is a full-time writer. She enjoys learning new things and writing about them. She lives with her husband and goofy golden retriever in Rhode Island. She has three grown daughters.

About the Illustrator

Rowan Barnes-Murphy has created images and characters for children's and adults' books. His drawings have appeared in magazines and newspapers all over the world. He's even drawn for greeting cards and board games. He lives and works in Dorset, in southwest England, and spends time in rural France, where he works in an ancient farmhouse.

Miss Singh, Tomás and Mia's teacher, trotted up to the lemonade stand. "Hi, everyone!" She waited for Mr. Smith, the softball coach, to get his lemonade. "I am so thirsty," she said. "I don't have any **cash**. Will you take a **check**?"

"Will we still get our money?" asked Mia.

"Of course," said Miss Singh. "Deposit it just as you would cash. Sign the back of the check. The bank will put the money in your account."

"How does a check work?" asked Tomás.

"That's a good question," said Mr. Smith. The bank will take money out of Miss Singh's checking account to give to you."

A check can be deposited into a checking account or a savings account. It can also be cashed.

"What if we don't go to Miss Singh's bank?" asked Mia. "Can we still deposit her check?"

"Yes. Banks talk to each other through the **Federal Reserve**," Mr. Smith explained. "It's a group of banks that govern banking for the United States. It will make sure that the money Miss Singh is paying you is taken from her bank and gets to your bank."

"Do all checks look like this?" asked Mia.

"Yes, they all look basically the same," said Miss Singh. "Checks can have different designs, such as cartoon characters or flowers. But they all have the same instructions for the bank. This check tells the bank who I am, that I'm writing the check to you, and the amount I'm giving you."

"Why write a check?" asked Mia. "Why don't you just use cash?"

"A check is safer than cash," said Miss Singh. "If I lost cash, I probably wouldn't get it back. If my checkbook were lost or stolen, I'd close my checking account. That way, no one would be able to get my money. I'd open another account and get new checks for the new account."

A check has information about you, your account, and your bank printed on it. You fill in the date, the person or company being paid, and the amount—in numbers and in words. There's a line for your signature and a place to include a note.

"Can anyone write a check? Do you have to have a checking account to write a check?" asked Tomás.

Mr. Smith nodded. "Yes, you do."

"Tomás and I have savings accounts. Can we open checking accounts, too?" asked Mia.

"Probably not," said Miss Singh. "Banks usually have a minimum age requirement, such as 16 or 18. Some banks let younger kids open a checking account with their parents."

Tomás's Uncle Tito arrived to pick up Tomás and Mia.

"Can we stop at the bank on the way home?" Tomás showed his uncle the check.

"Sure," Uncle Tito replied. "I haven't used a check in a long time. I use my **debit card**."

"A debit card is like a check, except the money moves electronically," said Miss Singh.

"You mean no one has to go to the bank?" Tomás asked.

"That's right," said Uncle Tito. "I use my debit card to buy gas."

"I don't even have to go inside to the cashier," he continued. "When I insert my card at the pump, the station's computer reads it and sends a message to my bank to subtract the amount I spend from my account. That same amount is added to the gas station's account. It's very **convenient**."

"What about **credit cards**?" asked Tomás. "Aren't they like debit cards? They look like credit cards."

"Credit cards and debit cards look alike. But they are different in an important way," said Mr. Smith. "When you use a credit card, you aren't taking money from your account. You're borrowing money from the company that gave you the card. It's money you have to pay back."

Debit and credit cards are plastic. The front of the card has the bank's name, the cardholder's name and account number, and the card's **expiration date**. The back has a place for the cardholder's signature and a magnetic strip with information card machines can read.

"Each month, you'll receive a bill for the money you've borrowed using your credit card," added Miss Singh. "If you don't pay your entire bill each month, you will be charged **interest**."

"You have to be very careful with credit cards," Uncle Tito warned. "They make it easy to spend money."

"Sometimes, people get in trouble with credit cards," said Mr. Smith. "They spend more than they can afford. Soon, they have more debt than they can manage."

"So, why would anyone use a credit card?" asked Mia.

"Credit cards are safer than other forms of payment," said Miss Singh. "If your credit card is lost or stolen, you are protected. If you tell the credit card company as soon as you know the card is missing, you will not be responsible for the purchases you did not make."

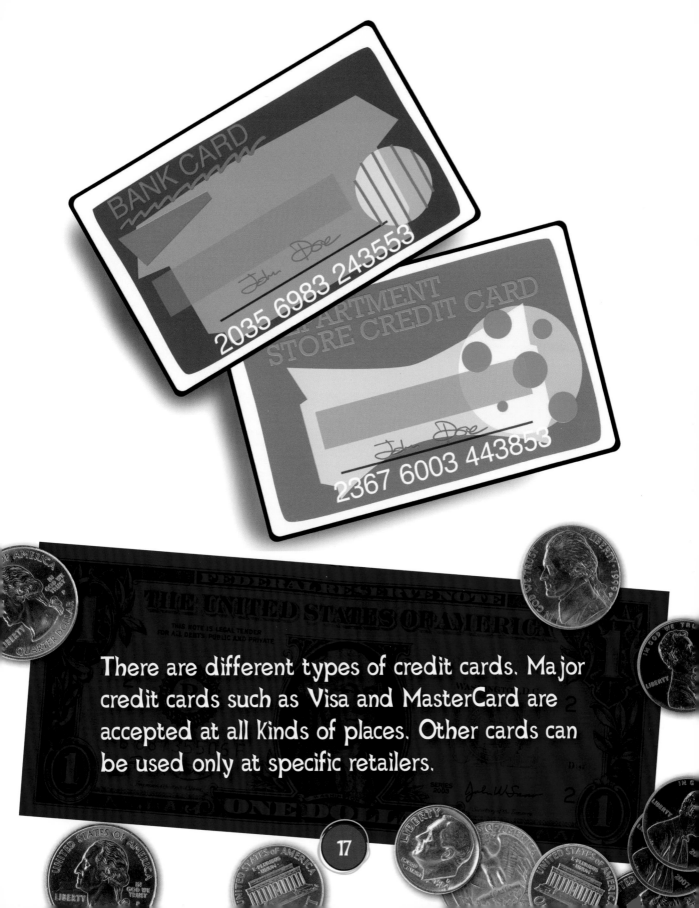

There are different types of credit cards. Major credit cards such as Visa and MasterCard are accepted at all kinds of places. Other cards can be used only at specific retailers.

"Credit cards are good in emergencies," added Uncle Tito. "When my car broke down, I didn't have enough money to fix it, but I needed my car. I put the repair charges on my credit card. And I paid them off quickly."

"Credit cards can also help you build a good credit history," said Mr. Smith. "Someday, you might need a loan to buy a car or a house. The bank will look at your credit history. If you paid your bills on time, the bank will be more likely to give you the loan."

"As long as you use them wisely, credit cards can be helpful," said Miss Singh.

"On the news, I heard about smart cards," said Tomás.

"Me, too," said Mr. Smith. "Those are credit cards with a tiny computer built in. This type of card requires the user to provide a special number to use the card. It's to protect against someone else using the card."

"Didn't someone build a machine that uses fingerprints like a credit card?" asked Mia.

"Yes," said Miss Singh. "Someday, we may not need cash or checks or cards at all. We'll just need these." She wiggled her fingers in the air.

"Whatever types of payment you use, you'll still want a money plan," said Tomás.

Mia nodded. "You bet! You still need to decide how much to spend, save, and give."

Glossary

cash (KASH): To exchange a check for money is to cash it. Cash is also the dollar bills and coins people use to pay for goods and services. Instead of depositing Miss Singh's check, Mia can cash it and get money in return.

check (CHEK): A check is a printed piece of paper with instructions for the bank to pay someone from your account. Miss Singh gave Mia a check for lemonade.

convenient (kuhn-VEEN-yuhnt): When something is convenient, it is useful or easy to use. Uncle Tito uses a debit card to buy gas because it's convenient.

credit card (KRED-it kahrd): This small, rectangular piece of plastic has information that is communicated electronically and allows the user to buy goods and services. Uncle Tito used a credit card to pay for his car repairs.

debit card (DEB-it kahrd): A plastic card that takes money out of your bank account to buy things is a debit card. Uncle Tito uses a debit card to buy gas.

expiration date (ek-spuh-RAY-shuhn date): The expiration date is when something can no longer be used. Credit cards have an expiration date.

Federal Reserve (FED-ur-uhl ri-ZURV): The Federal Reserve is a group of 12 banks that govern banking in the United States. Checks go through the Federal Reserve.

interest (IN-trist): Interest is the percentage of money someone pays on a loan or earns from a savings account. Using a credit card is like taking out a loan and requires paying interest.

Books

Hall, Margaret. *Credit Cards and Checks*. Chicago: Heinemann Library, 2008.

Houghton, Gillian. *How Credit Cards Work*. New York: PowerKids, 2009.

Web Sites

Visit our Web site for links about payment methods:

childsworld.com/links

Note to Parents, Teachers, and Librarians: We routinely verify our Web links to make sure they are safe and active sites. So encourage your readers to check them out!

Index